THE ULTIMATE SACRIFICE

The Biography of Aziz'u'llah Ashjari
1930 - 1985

Compiled by
Mitra Idelkhani-Ashjari
and Daryush Ashjari

O one and only God, O matchless Creator.
Praised and glorified art Thou for having
placed this splendid crown upon the brow
of these helpless ones, and this mantle
of eternal glory on the shoulders
of these indigent ones.

The rays of Thy sanctity fell upon bodies
of clay and the lights of the world
of eternity shone forth.

A flame of Thy bestowal from the enkindled
fire appeared and gave the hearts eternal
life. Thanks be to Thee for this blessing and
this bestowal and this bounty with which
Thou hast distinguished these helpless ones.

Thou art the Generous, the
Merciful and the All-Loving.

'ABDU'L-BAHÁ

The Greatest Name symbol is an Arabic
calligraphic rendering of the invocation
Yá Bahá'u'l-Abhá or O Thou Glory of Glories!

Introduction

In recognition of all the loved ones of the Blessed Beauty who have sacrificed their lives for Him and His cause, we write this biography of our late father Aziz'u'llah Ashjari. A number of attempts have been made to write a biography for our father, some with conflicting recounts and information. In this biography our aims and intentions are to compile the work done by others and validate all the facts. Special gratitude and appreciation go to our dearly loved aunt, Mrs Aghdas Ashjari Latifi, who so lovingly, precisely and fluently recounted her memories of her brother, our father, Mr Aziz'u'llah Ashjari. Her recount was an absolute inspiration and provided the assistance needed to put this biography together. May her loving and fond memories last forever.

We also recognise the loving memories of several family members mentioned in this biography who have ascended to the Abhá Kingdom. We dearly cherish them all and remember their love and care.

Bahá'ís have been subjected to hardship, persecution and execution in Iran since the inception of the Bahá'í Faith in 1844. Over 200 Bahá'ís were executed between 1978 and 1998 alone. This is the story of one of those 200 innocent martyrs of the Bahá'í Faith. Martyrdom in the Bahá'í Faith is the act of sacrificing one's life in the service of humanity and in the name of God.

Index

Family Tree

Agha Mirza Abdul Hadi
(Great Grandfather) ——— Bee Bee Hakim
(Great Grandmother)

Mirza Javad
(Great Uncle)

Mirza Asad
(Great Uncle)

Mirza Mohammad
(Grand Father)

Mohammad Ali Ashjari
(Father)

Robabeh Kashfi
(Mother)

Aghdas
(Sister)

Aziz'u'llah

Amin'u'llah
(Brother)

Early Childhood

On October 14th, 1930 (Mehr 22nd 1309) in Karaj, Iran, a boy was born to Mohammad Ali; known as Mohammad Ali Ashjari and Robabeh Kashfi; known as Seyedeh Ashjari. He was named Aziz'u'llah, which translates to "the dear one of the Almighty". Mohammad and Robabeh had married in 1920 (1299) and decided shortly after to pioneer to the city of Karaj, a city near Iran's capital Tehran renowned for its fertile land and pleasant climate. Here they were soon recognised as prominent landowners. The young couple were blessed with their first child, a girl named Aghdas, who was born a few years before Aziz'u'llah came to their lives, and in 1933 (1312) their youngest child, a boy named Amin'u'llah was born.

Robabeh Ashjari

The Ashjari family have a deep-rooted connection with the Bábí and Bahá'í Faiths. The very first person in the family who declared his faith to the Bab was Agha Mirza Abdul Hadi, the paternal great grandfather of Aziz'u'llah Ashjari.

Agha Mirza was amongst the companions of Sayyid Kazim Rashti. Agha Mirza announced his faith to The Báb after he came to His Holy Presence in a dream. Further, Haji Sulayman Khan, a Bábí martyr, was a close relative of Robabeh. It should be mentioned that it was Haji Sulayman Khan who protected the remains of The Báb and his companion Anis after their execution in Tabriz. Haji Sulayman consulted with both Bahá'u'lláh and Mirza Musa, Bahá'u'lláh's brother, to send a messenger to Tabriz for the purpose of gathering, protecting and transferring the Holy remains of The Báb and Anis.

Aziz'u'llah enjoyed the loving kindness of his father up until the age of six and was raised as a Bahá'í child by his parents. His father, Mirza Mohammad, was a victim of poisoning by the enemies of the Faith and took his flight to The Abhá Kingdom at the tender age of thirty.

Aziz'u'llah Ashjari   *Aghdas Ashjari*   *Amin'u'llah Ashjari*

A Turn of Events

Robabeh was left to raise three young children on her own, a task she undertook with absolute love and dedication. Her ordeals were heightened by the escalating pressure from local government authorities to take over their land, leading to confiscation of her books and family portraits. For a period of three years, she faced considerable hardship and difficulty making ends meet while managing the daily dealings with the farmers working on her land. The mounting pressure forced her to take refuge with her business advisor, a man named Gholam Bagheri, whom she eventually married. For the first two years of this marriage Gholam was supportive of Robabeh and her three children, allowing them to take part in Bahá'í activities and to interact with the local Bahá'í community in Karaj, but shortly after he isolated them and turned them against the Faith, forcing them to instead attend the local mosque and practice Islam.

Around this period, another Bahá'í family headed by Mr Ahmmadaie migrated back to Karaj in need of refuge and a home after returning from Russia. Robabeh made available one of her properties to Mr Ahmmadaie and his family and requested in return that he look after the spiritual education of her three children and nurture the love of the Faith in their hearts. Robabeh recalls this time as a very blissful period in her life. However, her husband Gholam could not stand these new circumstances, and was furious after seeing the three children return from attending a local Bahá'í Feast. He proceeded to push the Ahmmadaie family to move out of the property and to leave the city of Karaj. By now Aghdas was only thirteen years old, however her young age did not stop Gholam from imposing an unwanted marriage on her and ceasing her education and studies.

The year after Aghdas was forcibly married, Gholam made Aziz'u'llah leave school and work on a farm and shortly after this young Amin'u'llah was also made to end his studies. Robabeh, frightened and grief-stricken, tearfully sought counsel from Mr Ahmmadaie, who was now living in Tehran. His guidance lead to both her sons joining the armed forces to escape the undesirable environment Gholam had set for them. To facilitate this both boys had their date of birth put back by a few years on their birth certificate. Thus, with the continuous help and guidance from Mr Ahmmadaie, both Aziz'u'llah and Amin'u'llah joined the military, where Aziz'u'llah worked in the pharmacy section of the army, and Amin'u'llah joined the air force where he went on to become a well-accomplished aircraft technician. Upon completion of 2 years of military service Aziz'u'llah returned to Karaj and resumed supporting his mother.

Moving to Tehran

While still living in Karaj, Gholam's constant pressure, belittlement and controlling nature forced Aziz'u'llah to leave home to the city of Tehran at the age of 21. During this period, he stayed at his cousin's house and entered a work partnership with a man called Taghi which continued for several years, and together they were able to set up a successful business. However, Taghi was a faithless drunk who constantly influenced Aziz'u'llah and steered him away from the right path. This undesirable behaviour was observed by Aziz'u'llah's mother and sister, and after further consultation with Mr Ahmmadaie they found a new place for Aziz'u'llah to stay, where he was accompanied by his brother Amin'u'llah shortly after. During this period Aziz'u'llah resumed his interactions with the local Bahá'í community. Amin'u'llah, now a well-established aircraft technician with the air force, met a delightful young Bahá'í girl, Miss Maliheh Sadeghian. Amin'u'llah and Maliheh got married and moved to a pioneering post to form a Local Spiritual Assembly. Amin'u'llah's separation from his brother opened the doors for Aziz'u'llah to seek companionship with Taghi and yet again he became derailed from the right path.

Through the Will of the Almighty, Gholam lived a short life and passed away. At this time Mr Ahmmadaie sought the opportunity to reach out to Aziz'u'llah and helped him to reconsider his path. He convinced Robabeh to relocate to Tehran to live with Aziz'u'llah, where she could further assist and guide him. Through Mr Ahmmadaie and Robabeh's persistant efforts, Aziz'u'llah once again reconnected with the Bahá'í Faith. He then moved a new home in the Solaymanieh district in Tehran, a region that needed pioneers. Aziz'u'llah built a three storey house in Solaymanieh and rented part of it to a man named Mr Abbas Idelkhani and his family. Aziz'u'llah and Abbas became good friends and were well involved with Bahá'í activities. Their friendship lasted till the end of their lives. Mr Abbas Idelkhani, after moving to a pioneering post in Zanjan city, became of one the recent martyrs of the Faith.

Two parallels, both opposing, drove Aziz'u'llah to different directions. From one side the local Bahá'ís nurtured and supported Aziz'u'llah while his ill intentioned work partner, Taghi, continuously influenced him to misbehave and derail his life. Through the influence of the enemies of the Faith and propelled by Taghi's ill intentions, Aziz'u'llah started to attend Bahá'í firesides with the intention to disrupt these activities. One of the firesides that he regularly attended was held by Mr Alavi, a scholar of the Faith, where Aziz'u'llah put forward inflammatory claims and arguments about the Faith. During one of these fireside meetings Aziz'u'llah posed a profound question to Mr Alavi to which he received a compelling reply that touched his heart. In return a question was presented to Aziz'u'llah by Mr Alavi to which he found no apparent answer.

It was at this meeting that Mr Alavi raised his walking stick and told Aziz'u'llah: *"I shall deal with you with this stick for all the nonsense you pose and the path you have chosen"*,

Aziz'u'llah replied: *"Sir, if I don't pose such questions how would I find the truth and gain the insight to provide answers to people who pose these questions to me?"*

Later that night, when Aziz'u'llah was alone he pondered upon the course of the events of that evening and came to the realisation of the truth and the gift that had been bestowed upon him. He made a pledge to himself to part from his undesirable ways and instead dedicate his life to the cause of Bahá'u'lláh and His servants.

Aziz'u'llah in his 20s

The Beginning of a New Journey

Aziz'u'llah increased his interactions and engagements with the local Bahá'í community. During a conference held in the neighbourhood of Chahar Sad Dastgah at Mr Fooladchi's house, Aziz'u'llah met a Bahá'í youth from Kerman named Heshmat'u'llah Moshrefzadeh who had moved to Tehran to further his studies. Heshmat'u'llah and Aziz'u'llah became

From left to right front row: Amin'u'llah, Aziz'u'llah and Heshmat'u'llah

Manijeh, Aziz'u'llah, Robabeh, Heshmat'u'llah and Behrokh

like brothers and struck a deep and profound friendship that carried on through to the end of their lives. A short period into this friendship Aziz'u'llah invited Heshmat'u'llah to move in with him and requested that his mother, Robabeh, look after them both. Robabeh treated Heshmat'u'llah as her own son and was very pleased and delighted to see a Bahá'í youth positively influence Aziz'u'llah.

A new chapter had started in the life of Aziz'u'llah, his work and faith affairs flourished, and his friendship with Heshmat'u'llah had strengthened. Robabeh was now very pleased with her son and very appreciative of Heshmat'u'llah and encouraged them both to find a suitable lady to marry and start a family.

Through Bahá'í activities and friends, Aziz'u'llah met and married a young woman named Miss Manijeh Mohammad Agha, the eldest daughter of Mrs Derakhshandeh Mohajerin and Mr Abbas Mohammad Agha. In parallel to this Heshmat'u'llah developed feelings for Aziz'u'llah's niece, Miss Behrokh Latifi, the daughter of Aghdas Ashjari (Latifi), and they too got married. After one and half years both newly wedded couples welcomed the birth of baby girl each to their lives. It was during this time that Heshmat'u'llah and Behrokh moved to the city of Abadan for work reasons. It was also during this time that upon the request of

Wedding photo of Manijeh and Aziz'u'llah

Aziz'u'llah, Manijeh, Mitra and Daryush

the National Assembly of Bahá'ís of Iran, Aziz'u'llah played a key role to form one of the five Local Spiritual Assemblies in Tehran in the Solaymanieh district.

God blessed Aziz'u'llah and Manijeh with two children. Mitra was born in 1961 (1339) and Daryush was born in 1963 (1342).

During the summer of 1980 (1359) Mitra got married to Mr Rahim Idelkhani, the youngest brother of Mr Abbas Idelkhani, martyr of the

Faith. This marriage was blessed with three children, Nima, Sahba and Tina.

Daryush married Miss Niloofar Samali in 1993 (1372) and they had two children, Amy and Jordan. Both Idelkhani and Ashjari

Photo taken at Mitra's and Rahim's wedding day
On right is Mr Abbas Idelkhani

families currently reside in Sydney, Australia and serve the Faith.

Aziz'u'llah and Manijeh both dedicated a significant portion of their lives to serve the Faith and support the local community members in Solaymanieh. This was done to such extent that they built a new house and dedicated an entire floor as the local Bahá'í centre. Their house soon became the local centre to hold 19-day Feasts, Assembly meetings and Bahá'í Holy Day celebrations and activities.

The local community at large, a community that was prominently muslim, did not take to this positively, resulting in ongoing harassment, profanity and targeted disruptions from the enemies of the Faith.

Aziz'u'llah had an established mosaic factory in this neighbourhood, which was constantly targeted and destroyed with deep hatred and anger. They collapsed walls, broke windows and destroyed mosaics. These ongoing attacks and hateful behaviour impacted factory workers who were all muslim and now against Aziz'u'llah's success, way of life and religion. One day while he was repairing some machinery, a heavy hydraulic pump structure was let loose to fall on Aziz'u'llah causing major injury to his spine and back, an injury that accompanied him until the end of his life. The targeted tyrannies and cruelties were ongoing. On one occasion a handmade bomb was placed under Aziz'u'llah's car, God willingly, he identified it and defused it with no harm to anyone. On another occasion his car was stolen, taken several kilometres away to the north mountains of Tehran and driven off a mountain top falling into the deep trenches. The car was unrecoverable and destroyed. In another instance his personal briefcase was stolen and his bank chequebook was used by the enemies of the Faith. With forged signatures they withdrew a significant amount of money, forcing him to bankruptcy.

Despite of all these tribulations and hardships Aziz'u'llah and Manijeh continued their dedication and service. Aziz'u'llah was appointed as the custodian of a property of the Faith in Tehran, Zamineh Varzesh, a place dedicated to the youth, used for sport and education. Aziz'u'llah served on the Local Assembly for several years and was elected as the delegate to the Bahá'í National Convention for several terms. He took an active part in teaching and supported activities in the region.

National Convention BE 134 - Hadigheh Bahá'í Centre north of Tehran

Pioneering Opportunity

During the 1950s, the beloved Guardian had constantly encouraged Bahá'ís of Iran, and particularly Bahá'ís of Tehran, to take part in pioneering posts, both nationally and internationally. It was during this period that Aziz'u'llah made a pledge to his Beloved to pioneer and serve the cause of God where ever it was needed. He contemplated pioneering to Africa, however circumstances forced him to decide otherwise. Aziz'u'llah followed a traditional custom to meditate and pray for 40 nights and seek guidance of the Blessed Beauty to guide and direct him to the next chapter of his life. His verbal prayers and utterances were heard and noticed by all in the household and even neighbours. One night after meditation and prayers Aziz'u'llah found himself in the presence of the Beloved Guardian in a dream. The Guardian pointed to him and instructed him to hastily go to Tabriz.

In the morning, feeling dazed by this dream and after consulting with Auxiliary Board Member Mr Masih Farhangi, he set foot for Tabriz on the very same day. This was during the fasting period, the month of Ramadan, so no food or drink was available during the long 12-hour journey. Upon arrival to Tabriz and locating the house of the secretary of the Local Assembly, he received an unwelcome reception with remarks that Tabriz has over 220 local Bahá'ís and that there was no need for him in this city. However, he was informed that a nearby city, by the name of Ardabil, around 220 kilometres away, needed two Bahá'ís to form the local Assembly, and that perhaps he may wish to go there. Aziz'u'llah sought refuge in an abandoned yard, fed himself with a few simple cookies and found the way to travel to Ardabil. It was very late in the evening when he arrived and after he inquired with the locals, he located

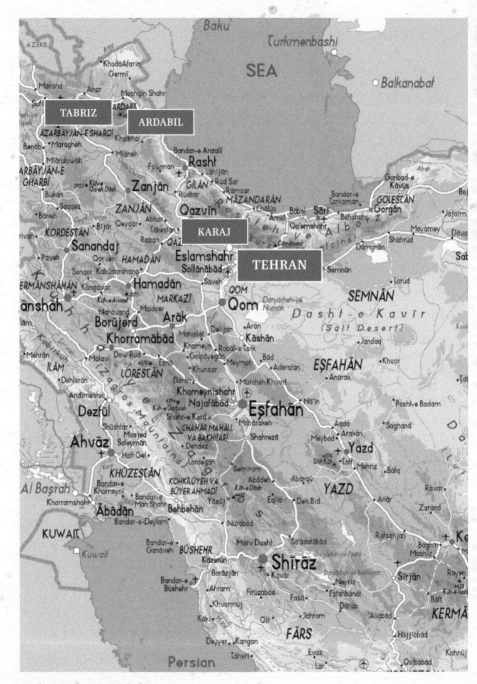

The four cities Aziz'u'llah lived in

the Bahá'í Centre. Aziz'u'llah stayed a few days in Ardabil and received a very warm welcome from the local believers. Now, set and assured that the request and guidance of the beloved Guardian has manifested itself, he returned to Tehran and started the process to move his family to this remote pioneering post. With the help and assistance of Mr Peyravi he rented a place in Ardabil, left his house and factory in Tehran for others to manage, packed his belongings and moved his family to Ardabil.

The Local Spiritual Assembly of Ardabil formed shortly after the arrival of Aziz'u'llah and Manijeh. Aziz'u'llah dedicated his entire time and effort towards supporting the local Bahá'í community and the affairs of the Faith in Ardabil and its nearby cities and villages. Aziz'u'llah, Manijeh and their two children had to go through a significant change to adapt to this new life. Ardabil is located within the East Azerbaijan state, a region where locals speak Turkish and were not fond of Farsi speaking people. As Ardabil is situated in between several mountains, it had a very cold, Siberian-like climate, where the temperature could drop as low as -25 degrees Celsius during the winter and a typical winter lasts 8 months with at least 6 months of snowfall. Life was harsh but the bond between the four members of Ashjari family was extremely tight, loving, and cheerful.

Their endeavours were encouraged and supported by Aziz'u'llah and Manijeh and backed by Divine guidance and blessings.

Aziz'u'llah visiting Bahá'í children in a small village

Life in Ardabil

Aziz'u'llah was appointed as the Assistant for Protection and Teaching a short while after he pioneered to Ardabil. This started a whole new environment for him and his family. Constant short trips to surrounding cities, towns, and villages, supporting the small group of Bahá'ís in these locations. He showed them the love and support of the Faith and the Institutions, hosting them at the family house when help was needed, particularly when they required medical and financial support.

As Aziz'u'llah enjoyed and loved nature, the untapped and uninterrupted natural beauty during these travels was blissful for him. Aziz'u'llah and Manijeh continued this life of service up until 1979 when the entire country went through an undesirable turn.

During 1977-78 the conditions for the local Bahá'ís started to shift and deteriorate. The Local and National Assemblies were forced to dissolve and a whole new wave of persecutions arrived

Aziz'u'llah and family visiting
Bahá'í Summer School in Tabriz

at the door of most Bahá'ís. The local Bahá'í members of Ardabil were under particularly substantial hardship and persecution. Soon it was not safe to hold Bahá'í activities; the local Bahá'í Centre was confiscated; most members fled and left and some even denounced their faith.

The newly formed revolutionary guards came to Aziz'u'llah and Manijeh's house and confiscated all Bahá'í books, magazines, family photos and any artifact that had to do with the Faith, appearing with undesirable tone and profanity. Soon after, the horrifying news was received that several members of the Local Spiritual Assembly of Tabriz had been executed.

True Destiny and Desire

On 17th of July 1981, 26th of Tir 1360, four members of the revolutionary guard arrested Aziz'u'llah, and he was taken to a local prison. The local prison warden, a friendly man towards Bahá'ís, was kind to Aziz'u'llah during the short period he was imprisoned in Ardabil. When the local prison warden came to know that a transfer request has come to relocate Aziz'u'llah to Tabriz, he gave Aziz'u'llah an opportunity to escape the prison. Aziz'u'llah thanked him and said that he was submissive to the law of the land and what has been ordered for him and that he was inclined to stay. His family was given permission to visit Aziz'u'llah on that same day where they spent several hours together for the very last time. After 25 days, on 11th of August 1981, Aziz'u'llah was transferred to Tabriz Jail, a prison located not far from the square where the Holy Bab and Anis where executed. Upon arrival to Tabriz Jail Aziz'u'llah was welcomed with 200 lashes on his back while his eyes where covered and then transferred to a solitary confinement cell

Aziz'u'llah at the courtyard of Tabriz prison

without any sleeping facilities. Aziz'u'llah spent a month in that horrible cell and then was transferred to another dark solitary confinement that contained only a single bed. After 5 long months, Aziz'u'llah was again transferred to the general ward amongst the worst criminals of the city. He was interrogated three times during this period, where he was subjected to verbal abuse, profanity, and mistreatment. He was accused of thirty eight counts of crimes against Islam.

During this period his family was denied any face-to-face visitations. At best a ten-minute weekly Sunday visitation was allowed through a glass window and over a closed-circuit phone. Limited supplies such as personal clothing items and food were allowed to be passed on to him after a thorough search and inspection by prison guards.

Due to ongoing threats, Manijeh and her son Daryush relocated to Tehran and stayed with Mitra and her husband Rahim. Daryush escaped Iran to Pakistan in 1982 and after fourteen months moved to Australia as a refugee immigrant.

بنام حق

Aziz'u'llah personal letter to Manijeh appreciating her efforts and visits

Manijeh displayed and portrayed absolute sacrifice and love towards her husband during this period. While being supported by Mitra and her husband, she travelled over 1500 kilometres round trip on a weekly basis to go and visit Aziz'u'llah for only ten minutes and supplied him with essential food items and clothing. Nothing deterred Manijeh from stopping her weekly visits, despite the long overnight journey, harsh and bitter winter weather and road closures... nothing could stop her from going to see her love. During this period which lasted more than four years, a number of Bahá'í friends in Tabriz helped to support Manijeh.

Aziz'u'llah was held at section 6 of Tabriz Jail. Several other Bahá'ís were imprisoned in the same jail and here they provided support and companionship to each other. Amongst them were Mr Jalal Peyravi, Mr Moosavi, Mr Zia'u'llah Oskooi, Mr Alireza Nikan, Mr Zekr'u'llah Fani and Mr Alizadeh.

In one afternoon, the entire group of Bahá'ís in Tabriz Jail were summoned for an interrogation session. They came to notice that a young Bahá'í man, Faramarz Dehghan, has been added to this group. Faramarz was not in a good physical condition but with the help and support of other Bahá'í prisoners he soon became better.

Around this time Aziz'u'llah pleaded to the prison warden to allow an hour of open air for daily exercise which was granted. When the prison warden came to understand that Aziz'u'llah

was a sportsman and a wrestler during his youth, he requested Aziz'u'llah become the football coach for the prison team.

Aziz'u'llah observing a prison football game

In 1984 (1363) Aziz'u'llah coached the wrestling team and subsequently in 1985 (1364) he coached the football team. Aziz'u'llah and other Bahá'ís in Tabriz Jail gained the respect and trust of the warden and his officers. As a result Aziz'u'llah, during his last year of imprisonment, was put in charge of the incoming and the outgoing mail for the prisoners.

Aziz'u'llah receiving a football trophy

23

مسابقات فوتبال بین زندانیان تبریز

Articles covering achievements of prison football team in local newspapers

یکدوره مسابقه فوتبال گل کوچک با شرکت ۱۰ تیم متشکل از بندهای سه‌گانه، موقت، شهربانی و دادسرای کمیته مستقر در زندان، بزرگداشت خاطره شهدای هفتم تیر بمناسبت دو گروه ۵ تیمی در محوطه بند موقت برگزار گردید.

در جریان دیدارها تیمهای سه‌گانه الف و بند موقت بند ۱ گروه... شکست دادن رقبای...

راد، محمد مولا، رحیم بعضلعلی‌پور و حمید علمداری (مربی) محبوب فرم ضیاء الدینی)

تیم بند موقت: شمس‌الدین سری، سید رضا مولوی هروی، یعقوب احمدی ناجی، رضا همران داد بخش و رسول حامدی (مربی - آشجاری)

تیم سه‌گانه بداهامبر اشرافی، اکبر عسگری، محمد رضا مهرابی، عفت‌رضا تازه کندی و محمد...

... گفتگوی کوتاهی عبدالله مسئول ورزش

... مالیتهای ورزشی در

دستگاه، سابقه بعنوان ... الا امکان سنتی ما ... کمبودها، وسیله ... بنا بر این در حال ... باشند می‌توانند ... جون باستانی ... وتبال بپردازند. ... نوانیم در این ... ن تیمهای ... ما همراه ... لاقه دارند سه ... ن توانستیم ... ولیس کشور

هت: اگر ... بیشتری ... گیرد، بگذارند.

بازیکنان تیمهای ندامتگاه تبریز به اتخذی

باج عبدالله نماینده دادستانی و نوروزی رئیس انجمن حمایت از زندانیان دیده می‌شوند.

است به سالن سرپوشیده تبدیل کنیم تا از این رهگذر بتوانیم به فعالیتهای بیشتری در امر ورزش ندامتگاه بپردازیم.

در حاشیه...

این مسابقات که در محوطه بند موقت انجام می‌گرفت، زندانیان دور تا دور محوطه نشسته بازی را نظاره می‌کردند.

در این میان عده‌ای که خوش ذوق‌تر از بقیه بودند، بساط چائی را نیز پهن کرده بودند، با اینکه گاهی توپ بازیکنان کاسه کوزمشان را بهم می‌ریخت، اما چاره‌ای جز خنده نداشتند. بالاخره

از قدیم گفته‌اند هرچی از دوست رسد نیکوست حتی اگر توپ باشه!!

هنگامی که عظیمی عکاس مجله می‌خواست از تیمها بگیرد عکس، مقابل دوربین هم دیده می‌شدند الا فوتبالیستها! چون دیگر زندانیان نیز علاقه داشتند، همراه بازیکنان عکسی به یادگار داشته باشند.

در آغاز دیدار دو تیم بند سه‌گانه الف و موقت با اینکه مسابقات در محوطه بند موقت میگرفت اما هیچگونه صدای تشویقی شنیده نمی‌شد. با اینکه هوا ابری بود و از آفتاب هم خبری نبود. اما بالاخره یخهای آب شد و به تشویق تیم خودی پرداختند، ولی زمانی به انکار مبادرت کردند که دیگر کار از کار گذشته بود. بقول معروف (علی مانده و حوضش) چون سه‌گانه الف بازی را یک بر صفر به نفع خود خاتمه داده بود.

24

Aziz'u'llah, accompanied by other Bahá'í prisoners were summoned for the fourth time to have a court hearing.

Eight of the prisoners received a two-year jail sentence, after already being in jail for four years. Aziz'u'llah, Mr Payravi and Mr Alizadeh left the court yet again after four years in prison, uncertain about their future. Soon after, the execution orders for Mr Payravi and Mr Alizadeh were announced.

These dedicated servants of Bahá'u'lláh happily and joyously accepted their death sentence with open arms and were martyred in Tabriz Jail. The impact of this act was so significant and impactful on Aziz'u'llah and other Bahá'í prisoners. They had no choice to accept the uncertainty of the situation and longed that perhaps they too would soon get to drink from the cup of sacrifice, if God was willing.

The Ultimate Sacrifice

On the 17th of November 1985 (26th of Aban 1364), for the first and the last time Aziz'u'llah was given the opportunity to see his close family face-to-face. After pleading with the officers, permission was granted for Manijeh, Mitra and her husband and their two children to visit Aziz'u'llah. They all assumed this was a positive sign and set off to travel to Tabriz to see Aziz'u'llah after over four years without seeing him in person. Upon arrival they were guided to a private room and soon after Aziz'u'llah joined them. This was a joyous and extremely emotional and happy occasion for all. Aziz'u'llah got to see his two grandsons, Nima and Sahba, and embraced and kissed them for the very first and last time. Aziz'u'llah showed signs of remorse and rejection, he cried that perhaps the Blessed Beauty has denied him the ultimate sacrifice. Visitation lasted forty-five minutes, giving all of them ample time and a long-awaited opportunity to talk and enjoy his company. In his last words to his family Aziz'u'llah said;

"Now that I have seen my loved ones I pray and beg Bahá'u'lláh to accept my blood and life for the progress of His cause, I have no further wish".

During the entire visit a clergyman was sitting in the room listening and observing them. Aziz'u'llah addressed him with respect and humility, and thanked him for this opportunity and special treatment. He turned around and looked at his loved ones and left the room. Manijeh, Mitra, Rahim and their two sons, Nima and Sahba, now uplifted after this visit returned to Tehran.

The very next day, a Monday, Aziz'u'llah's execution order was issued and shared with him. Aziz'u'llah took a pen and wrote his final wishes and will with no sign of hesitation, fear, or anxiety, and sought the forgiveness of his family and friends. The execution order of Aziz'u'llah had been issued two weeks prior and although the prison warden and officers knew of it, they could not bring themselves to accept and share it with Aziz'u'llah and the other prisoners.

At 9pm, on 19th of November 1985, 28th Aban 1364, Aziz'u'llah came to realise his ultimate wish and desire, and drank from the cup of martyrdom.

The following day, a prison guard reached out to local Bahá'ís and stated that Aziz'u'llah was unwell, asking them to inform his family to come to Tabriz. A telephone message was relayed to Manijeh from Bahá'í friends in Tabriz. An immediate feeling overcame Manijeh that "My dear one has obtained his wish and reached the destiny he longed for".

Manijeh, accompanied with her son-in-law Rahim and a few other relatives and close friends set to go to Tabriz.

On 21st of November 1985, 30th Aban 1364, Aziz'u'llah's physical remains were handed to his family and buried at a cemetery in Tabriz.

Aziz'u'llah's execution order was carried out with 3 gunshots to his abdomen and a final gunshot to his forehead.

هُوَ اللهُ

رَبَّنَا وَمَلاذَنَا أَزِلْ كُرُوبَنَا بِبُزُوغ شَمْسِ وَعْدِكَ الكَرِيمِ وَخَفِّفْ هُمُومَنَا بِنُزُولِ مَلائِكَةِ نَصْرِكَ المُبِينِ وَأَنِرْ أَبْصَارَنَا بِمُشَاهَدَةِ آيَاتِ أَمْرِكَ العَظِيمِ. رَبَّنَا أَفْرِغْ عَلَيْنَا صَبْراً مِنْ لَدُنْكَ. رَبَّنَا افْتَحْ عَلَى وُجُوهِنَا أَبْوَابَ السَّعَادَةِ وَالرَّخَاءِ وَأَذِقْنَا حَلاوَةَ الهَنَاءِ وَارْفَعْنَا مَقَاماً أَنْتَ أَوْعَدْتَنَا بِهِ فِي صُحُفِكَ وَكُتُبِكَ. إِلَى مَتَى يا إِلَهَنا هَذَا الظُّلْمُ وَالطُّغْيَانُ، إِلَى مَتَى هَذَا الجَوْرُ وَالعُدْوَانُ. هَلْ لَنَا مِنْ مَأْمَنٍ إِلاَّ أَنْتَ، لا وَحَضْرَةِ رَحْمَانِيَّتِكَ. أَنْتَ مُجِيرُ المُضْطَرِّينَ، أَنْتَ سَمِيعُ دُعَاءِ المَلْهُوفِينَ، أَدْرِكْنَا بِفَضْلِكَ يا رَبَّنَا الأَبْهى وَلا تُخَيِّبْ آمَالَنَا يا مَقْصُودَ العَالَمِينَ. وَأَرْحَمَ الرَّاحِمِينَ.

بنده آستانش شوقي

ای رَبّ توانا، تو شاهدی که در این لیلهٔ لیلا بر این عاشقانِ بینوا چه وارد گشته و در این سالیانِ دراز از حینِ مُفارقتِ وَجه صَبیحَت به چه سوز و گُدازی اهلِ راز دمساز. ای مولای قَدیر، اُفتادگی و بیچارگی آوارگانِ کویَت را مَپسَند و به شَدیدالقُوی این مُشت ضُعَفا را تأئید کن، در اَنجُمَنِ عالم عزیزانت را عزیز و مقتدر فرما و به تَحَقُّقِ آمال، این بال و پَر شِکستگان را سَرافراز و مُفتَخَر کن تا در این چند روزهٔ حیات عزّت و رفعتِ آئینت را به دیدهٔ عُنصُری بنگریم و به قلبی شاد و روحی مُستَبشَر به سوی تو پرواز کنیم.

تو دانی که نام و نشانی بعد از تو نخواهیم و سُرور و شادمانی و کامرانی در این عالَمِ فانی دیگر آرزو ننمائیم، پس وَعدَت را وَفا نما و جان و روانِ این خَسته‌دلان را نشئهای تازه بخش. دیدهٔ انتظار را روشن کن و جُرح قلوبِ گَئیبَه را التیام ده، به سَر منزلِ مَقصود کاروان‌های مَدینهٔ عشقت را به زودی برسان و به ساحتِ وصالت دردمندانِ هِجرَت را بِکشان زیرا در این عالَمِ اَدنی جُز ظَفَر و نُصرتِ اَمرَت را نخواهیم و در جِوارِ رحمتِ کُبری جز امیدِ وَصالَت آمالی در دل نداشته و نداریم.

توئی گواه توئی ملجاء و پناه، توئی نصرت‌دهنده این جمع بی‌گناه.

بندهٔ آستانش شوقی

The Final Will and Testament of Aziz'u'llah Ashjari *(Translated)*

"I, Aziz'u'llah Ashjari, son of Muhammad Ali, birth certificate number 1208 issued from Karaj, at this hour that death is arriving, in complete health and sanity write my final will.

My dear wife Manijeh, it is my wish that you continue to support and love Daryush and Mitra, now you need to be a father for them too.

Tell my son Daryush that I was happy with him and I hope that he continues and furthers his studies as much as he can to enable him to serve humanity and this Mighty Cause.

My dearest children, I embrace you and kiss your faces from the long distance and declare that I have prayed for your wellbeing every day and night.

My Mitra, at this last minute of my earthly life I put wellbeing and care of your mother in your safe, trusting and loving hands and I entrust you to the care of the Almighty God. Look well after your children, give utmost care to their education and upbringing.

My dearest and kind Rahim, I entrust my beloved Manijeh in your care and hope that you can look after her till the end of her life, she is my dear one and now entrusted to your loving care. May the Blessed Beauty reward you for all the kindness.

My dear Mitra, Rahim and Daryush, I embrace you and kiss you.

My kindest Manijeh, I am so thankful that I got to see you face to face yesterday. We shall reunite again in the Abha kingdom. I have left my watch, personal items and some money with the prison office, please collect them.

My dearly loved wife, be assured that I have been thinking of you till the last breath of my life and have been faithful to you and your pure love, I am proud of you. Don't be upset after my passing, say prayers for me instead of shedding tears. Look after my dear Daryush. You are free to determine the course of your life, seek help and always consult with Rahim. Do not be sorrowful about me.

God bestowed the best gift upon me yesterday to see you once more. I wish you health, happiness and new opportunities, my dearest, my kind love.

Aziz'u'llah Ashjari

The final will of Aziz'u'llah Ashjari, written a few minutes before his execution

اینجانب عزیزاله انصاری خورنده محمدعلی مشتاقنده شماره ۱۲۰۸ صادره از کرج در این ساعت

اول ماه ترک ذی الحجه ۰۰ با سلامت کامل وصیت مینمایم

عمده بام میرزه جان آنزده وندم که یا رو یا به دار دیگر همچنان ها در را خانه ا بخار بوم در اطلب نمانی

در حرمت لامکان به دار دیگر خوانده گوش کم به باید که این ای مالم بره دلیم دارم که تا آنگاه که مقدور است

تحصیل ادامه دهی تا همه بیوان ان به عالم شریت خدمت کنی خوانده ام از دو روز فرما این دارم و

عدل مهرو روش تا آخرین رضایی عمرم راست دعا میکنم هرا هنر دراین دقیقه گذر عمر مان

را ابرو بسپارم وکه را انداده ندیدم ام بزرگ انزها ذب گذار برنا دو در بست ذونا کوش بانی این

عزیز بدم نام میرزه جان را تو بسپارم ولیه دارم که با آخر عمر مراطلب دو ها ادا مانشت مناشیم

برشت وشارا بحق بخی علام جبدم (میراجان منم در دار دیگر به ویان دیم ویسوندیمان)

هرده نام میرزه جان دراین دم آخر عمر روز قبل که اطلاعات در یا رست مردم و دو دید مالک

بهتر بعد بیشگاه خانه شمال هرم ساعت سبیک ۱۸۰۰ سال که مردم راست براین نکویل گیر

بین را که هنده تقضیه نفر زندان مراکسی دیگر مثلی مربع دم و ها از نفر زندان گیر مطلع ۶ هزار نفر

۲ دلی را دار بگیر هرم هان هان هیه با آخرین دقیقه عمرم بیا دو دیرم و عتی برگ تو انفتار

مهروان فرادتر کم با حت ناز در کار کی و دیران سرایم لماکی و مناحت کوانی دارد

پارکزی ماح بهون بهوع بنتگی هم هرو بهت میدانی ماک کیم غمیر اقدام نما وکل بنتگی با حم حرد

ی ولاز جانب من هیورد ناحت نای لمدر خانه آنه رف بت دارنا آخرین روزها عمر حکرد

انزلیک به بینم در خانه سعادت و سلامت و نعمت کر همسر مرزه دعیزم از بام راخوان ین

The next day Manijeh and Rahim went to the prison to claim and collect the personal belongings of Aziz'u'llah. Officers denied the request. Rahim persevered with the officers, pleading that Aziz'u'llah's son is overseas and a note or will written by him would be of significant value. The officers eventually accepted and handed over a personal diary, a few clothing items, and the note that Aziz'u'llah was able to write at his last moment.

A page from the personal diary of Aziz'ullah

Until his last breath Aziz'u'llah was a thankful, obedient and a loyal servant of Bahá'u'lláh. He loved to study the writings, acquire more knowledge about the Faith and to memorise prayers. Even during the imprisonment period, he continued memorising and reciting tablets and prayers and exchanged them with his prison mates.

The in-person family visit gave Aziz'u'llah the opportunity to share the following remarks:

"Say prayers for me my loved ones, the end is undetermined, if I have the bounty, He shall summon me and take me, if not I will dedicate my life to serve the families of His martyrs, even till my last breath, this is my wish and desire."

"My final earthly desire was to see my grandchild, now I have no further wish but the acceptance of the will of my Beloved."

A week prior to his execution, during a football match a few photos were taken including a portrait photo of Aziz'u'llah. Aziz'u'llah shared that portrait with Manijeh during the in-person visit.

At the age of 57 Aziz'u'llah Ashjari, paid the ultimate price and sacrificed his life for his Beloved and the progress of His mighty Faith.

May his soul be ever joyous in the presence of the Blessed Beauty and his loved ones in the Abha Kingdom. May the warmth from the candle of his love warm our hearts forever.

Mitra Idelkhani-Ashjari & Daryush Ashjari - August 2022

A Personal Reflection

A few words from Aziz'u'llah's son
and daughter – Daryush and Mitra.

*Daryush together
with his lovely wife
Niloofar.*

Sydney Australia 2021

Dear Dad

It was a hot summer afternoon, I was three years old, you, Mitra and I were in the small pool in the middle of the backyard, throwing water at each other and laughing... This is the very first memory I can recall from you Dad. The sound of your voice and laughter echoes in my ears and I cast my mind back and see what a life you had, your legacy and how dedicated you were to your Faith.

Mitra and I learnt from you that we live to serve the Faith and humanity, everything else is second. I admire your deep involvement with all aspects of the Faith. I recall hearing your voice in the early mornings and sometimes late at night, reciting the long obligatory prayer. Later in life I came to realise that you taught me the long obligatory prayer that way and I am so grateful for that. I recall that every evening you had an engagement related to the work of the Faith and we did not see you during the weeknights. I recall your loving encouragement every Friday morning to usher us to the weekly Bahá'í children's class. I recall that one day, a Friday morning, I was heading back home from the Bahá'í children's class and got beaten up by local neighbourhood boys who called me a Bahá'í dog, I came home crying and you gave me refuge and comfort in your arm and told me that this is all for Bahá'u'lláh, and he will reward me for the obedience and any sacrifices I make. I recall how you and mum joyously and willingly served the local community, hosting daily meetings at our house. I recall your firesides and how you regularly met with youth in our community tackling their questions on how to promote and defend the Faith. I recall the turbulent and scary months of Moharram of Ramedan each year, where locals were fasting or mourning the martyrdom of Imam Housain. I recall how the large groups of Muslims gathered in front of our house during Ashora, chanting aloud, stomping on the ground and beating their chests with their hands showing animosity and hate to us. I recall seeing you fearlessly standing at the front of the house, like a lion, and staring them off. I recall how I longed to observe the fast with you when I was little, and you kept laughing and telling me "my dear your time will come soon".

I recall how tough and determined you were. You made me attend to chores that I did not want to do, at times I hated doing them. Now I see why! You made me resilient, confident and determined.

I recall our times when we pioneered to Ardabil. I enjoyed that period, we got to see you every day and be with you. I recall the short trips we had together visiting the small Bahá'í communities and individuals. I recall seeing the impact of those visits, the kindness that you and Mum showed to them all.

I recall a dream that I had when I was 16. Both beloved Bahá'u'lláh and 'Abdu'l-Bahá came to visit us at our home in Ardabil. 'Abdu'l-Bahá instructed me to dig the ground in the middle of our house, where a water stream started to flow. Soon after, he turned to you and said, this is divine water, drink it and share it with my beloved friends. I recall sharing this dream with you and you told me that it signifies why we came to this pioneering post and why we have to share the love of the Faith with everyone.

I loved that you made me so familiar with tools, cars and anything mechanical. You told me that I can fix anything as long as I act methodically and don't make it worse.

I recall pondering how you left a very successful and busy life in Tehran and moved to the small, remote and unwelcoming city of Ardabil. I kept asking myself the question, could we have served the Faith better if we lived in Tehran? But how wrong I was.

I was at Mitra's house in Karaj when the news reached us that you were arrested and soon after Rahim and I came to Ardabil to support mum. I recall, for the last time in my life, seeing you face-to-face while you were arrested in a detention centre, I recall holding you and covered in tears, you told me to be strong, put my entire energy to study and gaining knowledge and serve the faith, you told me to find a life partner that believes in Bahá'u'lláh and his Faith and serve the Faith together. I recall that you told me your watchful and supporting eyes will be always looking at me, and in the blink of an eye, I was denied from seeing you and holding you for ever.

In your last will you asked Mum to look after me and I assure you that she did till her last breath. She was the kindest, most loving and supporting mother that one could ask for.

Dad, I was denied a normal life and your guidance since I was 17. I have missed you every moment I am alone and the deep pain of losing you has never gone away, and the scar never healed. At a number of occasions, I have missed your presence intensely, particularly at my wedding ceremony with Niloofar and when Amy and Jordan were born.

Dad, I wish you could be here, even just for a few minutes, to meet Niloofar, Amy and Jordan. You would have loved them as I do and as Mum did. Niloofar is an angel, she loved mum and looked after her so much. I so hoped that you could have met Dr Manoocher Samali, Niloofar's father, he was a very special person in my life and treated me as his own son, a very devoted servant of Bahá'u'lláh.

Mum had a good life in Australia, I am certain you had a lot to do with it. She enjoyed her peace and independence. She enjoyed being with her 5 grandchildren and showered them with love, generosity and affection. She was so detached from earthly possessions and loved to give to others. We gave mum a very dignified and spiritual send-off when she passed away. Her resting place is only a few minutes away from us, I often go there and say prayers for you and her.

I have been blessed and supported throughout my life. I believe a mysterious force has been looking after me and protects me. I know you have something to do with it Dad. I have felt your presence and influence over my life, and I hope that it will continue. I hope you continue to look after Amy and Jordan and influence them similarly.

Earthly lives are limited and uncertain, how our physical lives come to an end is unknown but certain. Perhaps our circumstances could have been different, and we would have had you with us for much longer, but every physical life must come to an end. What a life you had Dad!

You lived a life of sacrifice and service, and I am certain Mitra and I could not have asked for anything more.

I hope you are proud of me for who I have become. I love you deeply and I miss you every day. I am honoured and humbled that the Almighty God blessed me to be your son, a son that is so delighted and proud of his martyred father.

Love you forever.

Your son Daryush

My dearest Dad (Baba Joonam),

It has been almost 37 years since I wrote my last letter to you and saw you in person for the first and last time during the whole five years of your imprisonment. I know my talks to you every night, to consult with you, ask for your guidance and help and pour my heart out to you, has never ended and will never end. This letter, as I am pondering on all my wonderful childhood memories, forces me to reach into memories etched in my mind and buried untold for so many years.

As long as I can remember you were our family's pillar of strength, wisdom and resilience. During my early childhood you were always busy with the Faith's activities which was your priority all throughout your life, but it didn't mean you'd forget about us. I loved attending your regular Friday morning dawn prayers for our community

Mitra and Husband Rahim - Sydney Australia

members, I remember seeing you sitting in your car at a distance watching me walk home with my friends and assure my safety as the Faith's enemies had threatened to harm our family. During the years when you were the caretaker of Baha'i Sport Centre in Tehran, we witnessed what your faith and your devoted service meant to you; even though we did not have much of your time and attention that often, but you tried to include us whenever possible. Such an occasion was when you had the duty to accompany Mr Movahed or Mr Bakhtavar to firesides and take them back to their homes and you took us with you. Our family's accompaniment would make the enemies of the Faith believe that a family affair is taking place and refrain from troubling them. Every aspect of our lives was amalgamated with service to our Faith. When you were finally able to purchase and renovate a Baha'i Centre in our local area, all your focus was to get the community members, especially the youth, to unite and serve in harmony.

Every year during the mourning month of Moharram, when our house was surrounded with opponents of the Faith, day and night, we were assured that you would protect us unconditionally. I remember how your enemies, on several occasions, stole your cars and destroyed them. Your factory was burnt down and even your workers provoked. Once they dropped very heavy machinery on your back while repairing it, injuring your lower back and consequently you suffered from it for the rest of your life.

When we agreed to go pioneering to the north-west of the country a city called Ardabil after your vivid dream, it was the hardest change in our lives. To be away from the rest of the family, circle of friends and school, was terribly hard for us but knowing we had you to support us and be with us, made it all worth while. Those were the best years of our lives.

After the revolution it was even harder for us to be away from family. On one occasion when guards came to search our house for Bahá'í books and materials, the first thing you did was to take me outside and lock me inside your car so none of them could harm me. I witnessed how brave and courageous you and mum were. They took all our books, cassette tapes, folders, magazines and anything that had to do with Bahá'í Faith, but they didn't know you had already outsmarted them and moved your precious 700+ books to a safe place. Reading these books was your pride and joy and you'll be happy to know after you were martyred, we gave them to the community to use as they were so rare and precious.

When I had decided to get married in 1980, the only thought on my mind was you, mum and Daryush's wellbeing in a very fanatic town, full of blind followers of a regime.

In early summer of 1981, you came to visit us in Tehran, I had just fallen pregnant with my twins Nima and Sama (Sama only lived for 3 days after birth) but you didn't know it then. I begged you not to go back to Ardabil as they had threatened to arrest you so often. But you reassured me, your destiny was to serve the Faith regardless of how it would end. I was six weeks pregnant with Nima and Sama when you were arrested upon your return to Ardabil. During the five years while you were in prison, they whipped you, left you in solitary confinement and interrogated you several times without any legal representatives in court. When they kept threatening to capture my little brother Daryush while you were in prison, with your approval my husband Rahim and I had relocated Mum and Daryush to our home in Fardis Karaj. However, that meant Mum had to travel for 12 hours on a weekly basis by public bus to see you in prison for only ten mins, behind a thick glass, over a phone and for this lonely lady to travel another 12 hours to come back home. The things this courageous woman went through for you was beyond anyone's belief and comprehension and I still cannot fathom how she did it for more than five years.

You specifically found it heart-warming knowing that Daryush had escaped Iran to migrate to Australia, even though it was hard to let go of your precious son, but you insisted that he needed to further his studies and get educated to be more useful to society as he could not go to university in Iran.

In all the hundreds of letters you wrote to us you constantly advised us to stay strong and support each other. Rearing my then 2 children in the cradle of Faith was so important to you. Being a fifth generation Babi/Bahá'í had given you a very strong sense of belief that nothing else came before the Faith. Your parents, siblings and you had made so many sacrifices, ultimately giving your life for your beloved religion.

When I was going through the last few weeks of my third pregnancy with Tina, my doctor had advised me that I am running out of time to travel long distances and I only had a week to do so. Mum suggested that we drive to Tabriz to visit you together, resulting that each one of us would get one to two minutes to talk to you. So Mum, our resilient mother, your most caring and faithful wife, went to seek permission from the authorities for a face to face visitation. She came back so happy holding a permission note, she said they didn't even question it. Very little did we know that this was the first, the only and the last time we were to see you in prison face to face.

We met in an office while a turbaned prison official was sitting behind a desk observing us. You were so pleased to finally see and hold your two grandsons, Nima and Sahba, and wished we would be blessed with a girl. With my last pregnancy your wish was granted as our little girl Tina was born 40 days after your martyrdom. As Nima grabbed a lolly from Mum's bag and gave it to you, you said this was the last wish you had and now you have fulfilled all your wishes and hopes, and you are ready for the privilege of giving your life for Bahá'u'lláh and his Cause. You mentioned to us that if you were to be released from the prison, you would dedicate rest of your life to the families of the Martyrs of the Faith and document what had happened to each and every one of them while in prison. I had never seen you cry before, but you were upset, crying that the Almighty did not give you the chance to sacrifice your life for Him. We were all so happy to spend 45 mins with you talking about things important to us.

We were on cloud nine driving back home thinking that the situation was getting better and easier. The very day after, someone approached Rahim telling him that a soldier from Tabriz prison has made contact asking a family member to go back to Tabriz with no reason given. As soon as mum heard this, she sat down and said "he's free now, they've killed him, I can feel it".

You were laid to rest a few days later but I was not able to attend your funeral as Mum and Rahim travelled to put you to rest but I have felt your presence in my life ever since.

Dad, my family has grown since then and we are blessed with two wonderful daughters-in-law and 4 gorgeous grand kids.

You finally got your wish dad, your ultimate wish. There is not a single day that goes by that I don't miss you. I am happy you were granted the permission to sacrifice your life for your beloved Faith. Please help and guide us, may we all get to serve and stay as strong as you did. Please help our family members stay faithful and make this world a better place.

Miss and love you eternally.

Forever your little girl,

Mimi

Special Images and Documents

Aziz'u'llah and Manijeh Ashjari

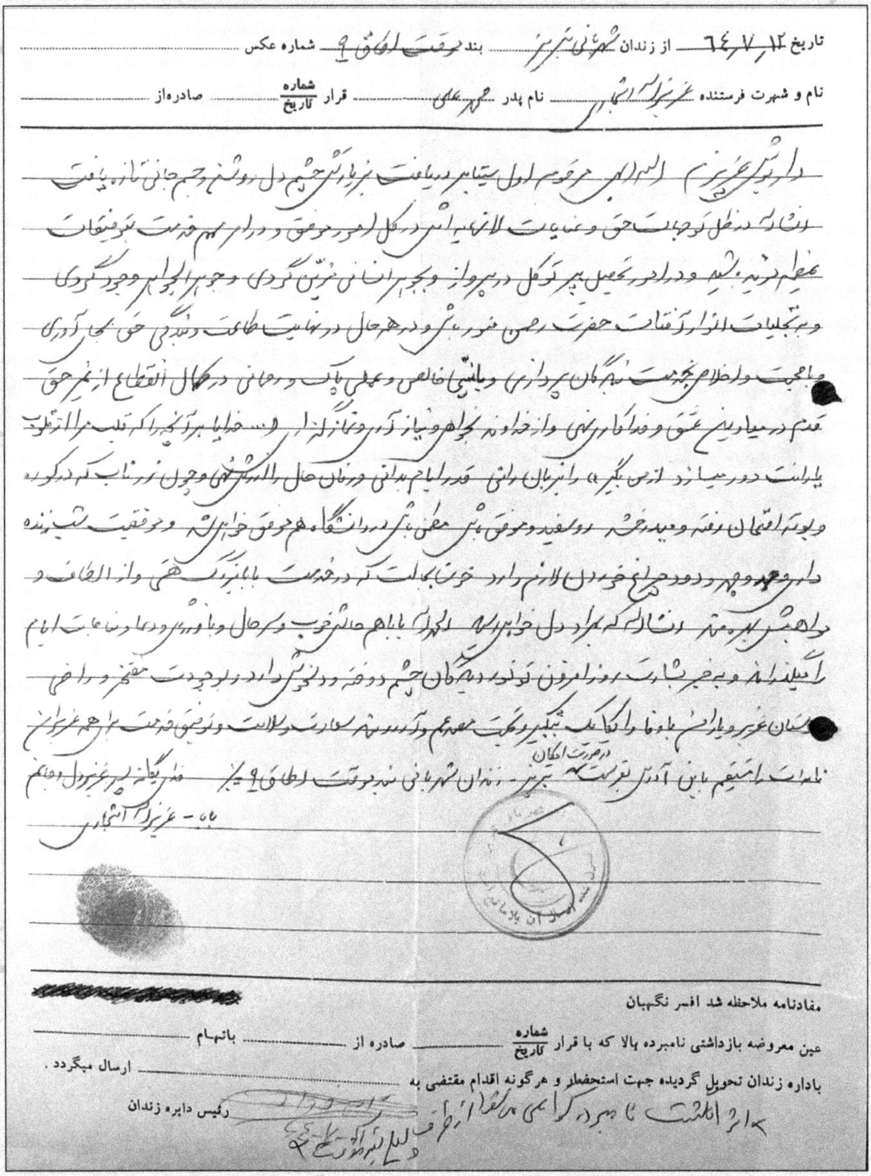

بسم الله الرحمن الرحیم

[متن دستنویس فارسی]

۱۰۰ ـ عزیزالله آشنایی

A personal letter to Daryush from
Aziz'u'llah while in prison

The gravestone Aziz'u'llah Ashjari
Tabriz Cemetery - Block 9, Row 7, No 26

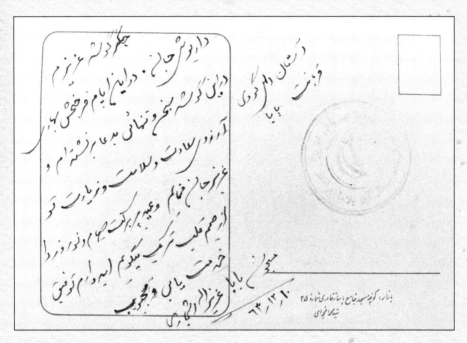

Postcard send to Daryush for the new year

۹/۱۱/۱۲۶۱

عزیزان میترا و داریوش و منیژه خانم گرانقدرم ... امیدوارم نفضو و مرحمت حق ...

در کمال ... سپردارم

تهران ش ...
۹/۱۱/۱۲۶۱

Letter to Mitra, Manijeh and Daryush

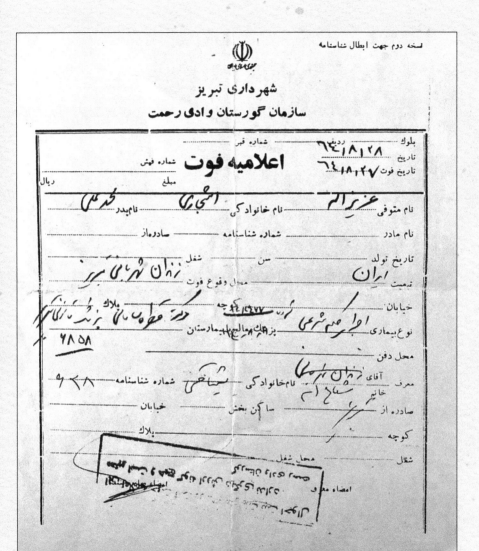

NATIONAL SPIRITUAL ASSEMBLY OF THE BAHÁ'ÍS OF AUSTRALIA
INCORPORATED

P.O. BOX 285, MONA VALE, N.S.W. 2103

PHONE: 913 2771
913 2772

CABLES: "NATBAHAI SYDNEY"

30th December, 1985.

MF 121.

Mr. Dariyush Ashjari,
Lane Cove.

Dearly Loved & Respected Friend,

The National Spiritual Assembly was shocked yet exhilarated when it
received a telex from the Universal House of Justice concerning the
martyrdom of Azizu'llah Ashjari. We know the deep personal sorrow
you are experiencing at the loss your noble loved-one but we, on the
National Assembly, during prayers in the House of Worships, experienced
something of the joy and exhilaration as another one of Baha'u'llah's
finest followers willingly gave his life for the Faith.

May you come to realize the bounties and boundless opportunities that
Azizu'llah has given to you by the sacrifice of his life for Baha'is
throughout the world.

In the Faith there is no greater glory than to offer your life that
others might live.

Even as we share your deepest sorrow so we share your joy.

With the love that only followers of the Glory can ever know.

The NATIONAL SPIRITUAL ASSEMBLY

OF THE BAHA'IS OF AUSTRALIA.

Ray Meyer,
Secretary.

*Letter of condolence from National
Spiritual Assembly of the Bahá'ís of
Australia*

A personal letter to, Mitra, Rahim, Daryush and Nima from Aziz'u'llah while in prison

Manijeh, Mitra and Daryush

Aziz'u'llah and Manijeh at Bahá'í holyland pilgrimage 1970

O MY GOD! O MY GOD!

Verily, thy servant, humble before the majesty of Thy divine supremacy, lowly at the door of Thy oneness, hath believed in Thee and in Thy verses, hath testified to Thy word, hath been enkindled with the fire of Thy love, hath been immersed in the depths of the ocean of Thy knowledge, hath been attracted by Thy breezes, hath relied upon Thee, hath turned his face to Thee, hath offered his supplications to Thee, and hath been assured of Thy pardon and forgiveness. He hath abandoned this mortal life and hath flown to the kingdom of immortality, yearning for the favour of meeting Thee.

O Lord, glorify his station, shelter him under the pavilion of Thy supreme mercy, cause him to enter Thy glorious paradise, and perpetuate his existence in Thine exalted rose garden, that he may plunge into the sea of light in the world of mysteries.

Verily, Thou art the Generous, the Powerful, the Forgiver and the Bestower.

'Abdu'l-Bahá

Lightning Source UK Ltd.
Milton Keynes UK
UKHW051453151022
410485UK00007B/20

9 781922 562999